Published by Christian Focus Publications Ltd
Geanies House, Fearn, Tain, Ross-shire IV20 1TW www.christianfocus.com

Copyright © John Brown Brian Wright
ISBN: 978-1-5271-1167-7

This edition published in 2024
Cover illustration and internal illustrations by Lisa Flanagan
Cover and internal design by Lisa Flanagan
Printed and bound by Imprint, India

All rights reserved. No part of this publication may be reproduced, stored in a retrieval system, or transmitted, in any form, by any means, electronic, mechanical, photocopying, recording or otherwise without the prior permission of the publisher or a licence permitting restricted copying. In the U.K. such licences are issued by the Copyright Licensing Agency, 4 Battlebridge Lane, London, SE1 2HX. www.cla.co.uk

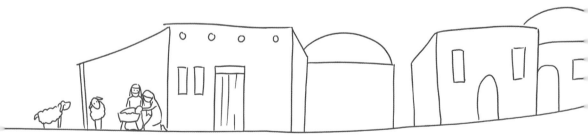

Micah's
~hope~

John Brown
Brian Wright

After King Solomon, but before King Jesus, God sent the prophet Micah to preach **judgment and hope** to His people.

"**Listen up!** Let everyone hear what God has to say!"
"**Look up! The Lord is coming!**
The mountains are melting! They are running like wax down into the fields, which have burst open!"
"**Why is this happening?**
Because of His people's sin."

"I will make the city of Samaria **a complete ruin.**"
"I will plow her streets, topple her walls,
smash her idols, and burn her treasures."

"The Assyrians will destroy Judah's towns as they march toward Jerusalem."

"'Dust-Town' should roll in the dust in grief."

"Vain 'Beauty-Town' will go shamefully into exile."

"The bold people of 'Go-Forth Town' will cower in fear."

"'Sweet-City' will become bitter."

"'Horseburg' should flee away on racehorses.

"Send farewell gifts to Brideville, for she is going away."

"Dry-Town', Israel's kings will get no relief from you."

"'Victorville,' you will be conquered, and your leaders will hide in caves."

"Oh, **people of Judah!** Show you're sad by shaving your heads, for your beloved children will be taken far away."

"**Woe to you** who scheme at night to steal by day."

"The Lord will **take from you** like you took from others."

"Your enemies will tease you and **take you away** as well."

"Stop saying these things, Micah!" said the people. "God won't let such bad things happen to us!"

"**Oh, yes He will!**" Micah replied.
"For you steal the shirts right off people's backs
and kick women out of their homes
and strip children of what God gave them."

"So **get up** and **get out!**
Your sin has ruined our land."

"But someday, O Israel, **I will gather** you like sheep,
and your land will again be loud with crowds."

"**The Lord your king** will rescue you from your
enemies and lead you back home."

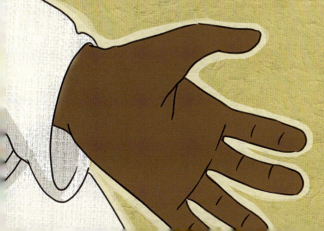

"**Listen up!** You leaders should know justice, but instead you hate good and love evil. Do you really expect God to help you after all the bad things you've done?"

"**You prophets** say good things to those who feed you but bad things to those who don't. Therefore God will stop showing you the future, and you will be ashamed."

"As for me, **the Spirit of the Lord** fills me with power and justice to speak against your sins."

"**You are all corrupt**, you leaders, prophets, and priests; you take bribes and teach and prophesy only for money."

"You think nothing bad will happen to you since you live near the Lord's temple."

"Yet because of you, Mount Zion will be plowed like a field, Jerusalem will be reduced to rubble, and tall trees will stand where the temple stood."

"But **in the last days,** the temple mount will be the most important place in the world."

"People will stream there to **worship** the Lord and to **learn** from God how to live."

"The Lord will establish **perfect peace.** Swords will be hammered into plows and spears into pruning hooks.

"Nations will **no longer fight** or train for war."

"**Everyone will thrive,**
and no one will be afraid, for everything will be good,
and there will be **nothing to fear."**

"The Lord of Heaven's armies has promised this, so we will only follow **the Lord our God** forever and ever."

"In that day I will **bring home** the sick and the sad and make my people strong again."

"From Jerusalem **I will rule** as their king forever."

"Now you cry out in fear,
for you have no king to lead you
or wise people to counsel you
as **your exile nears.**"

"But the Lord will **rescue you**
and **crush your enemies,**
and you will gratefully
give their wealth to the Lord.

"He will lead His flock with **the Lord's strength** in the majestic name of God."

"The whole world will **honor Him**, and He will establish **peace** for His people."

"**God's people** will be mighty among the nations, irresistible like the dew the Lord sends on the grass."

"They will be **strong like lions**, defeating their enemies."

"In that day," says the Lord, "I **will judge** the nations that refuse to obey Me."

"I will **defeat** their armies, **demolish** their fortresses, **dismiss** their sorcerers, and **destroy** their idols."

"**Listen up!**" says the Lord. "How could you reject and rebel against Me, after how good I've been to you?"

"I **rescued** you from Egypt, **protected** you from your enemies, **led** you through the wilderness, and **brought** you into the Promised Land."

"Time and again I've proven **My faithfulness** to you!"

"**What should we do** so that God will be pleased with us?"
"Should we sacrifice **thousands** of rams
and offer Him **ten thousand** rivers of olive oil?"

"No. The Lord has already told you **what is good** and
what He requires of you: Do justly, love mercy,
and **walk humbly** with your God."

"Be wise, Jerusalem, and fear the Lord!"

"He is sending armies to destroy you!"

"And why? Because your merchants are dishonest and cheat their customers."

"The rich hurt the poor, and your citizens lie so much, they can't even tell the truth anymore."

"I did this to prove **My faithfulness** to you!"

"I'm so sad!
It seems like there are no good people left."

"The leaders and judges **demand bribes**
and twist justice."

"**No one trusts** anyone anymore,
not even best friends or spouses."

"**Children defy parents**
and people have enemies in their own families."

"As for me, I look to the Lord for help and wait confidently for God to save me, for I know He hears my prayers."

"Don't laugh at me, for even if I fall,
I will rise again."

"Though things are dark right now,
the Lord is my light."

"He will raise me up, bring me into the light, and my enemies will see that **the Lord is on my side.**"

"In that day, Israel's **cities** will be **rebuilt** and its **borders extended.**"

"People from around the world will come to **honor you**, even those who used to be your enemies."

"The land of those who don't will become **deserted** and **devasted.**"

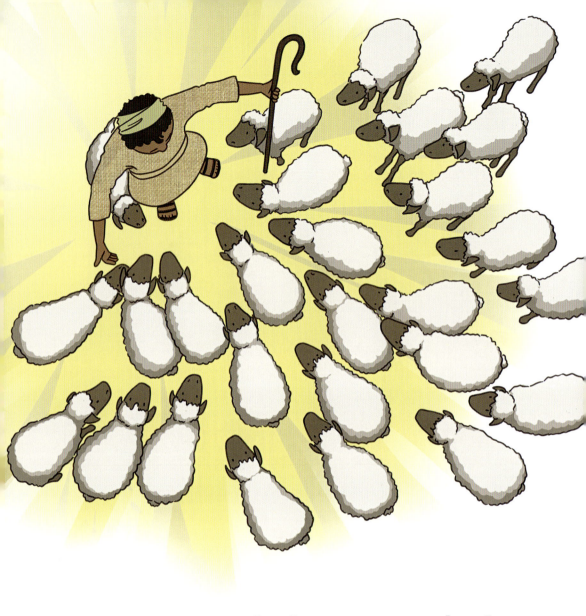

"O Lord, **protect** Your people and **lead** Your flock like a **shepherd**. Let them graze in green pastures like long ago."

"**I will**," says the Lord, "I will do mighty miracles for you like I did when I rescued Israel from slavery in Egypt."

"The nations will be **amazed** at what I do for you and will **fear the Lord**, trembling in His presence."

"Who is like You, O God, who **forgives** His people's **sins**?

"You do not stay angry with Your people forever because You delight to show **unfailing love.**"

"You show us **compassion** and trample our sins under Your feet and throw them into the ocean deeps."

"You are **faithful** and Your **love** never fails, just as You promised our ancestors Abraham and Jacob long ago."

Micah's name means, "**Who is like the Lord?**" Which really means, "No one is like the Lord!"

No one is so **compassionate** and **forgiving** as the Lord!

No one is so **faithful** and **loving** as the Lord!

The Lord proved this by sending His Son, Jesus, to **die** on the cross and **rise** from the dead to **save** us from our sins. And the Lord will send Jesus again to rule over His people in perfect peace **forever and ever!**

Christian Focus Publications publishes books for adults and children under its four main imprints: Christian Focus, CF4K, Mentor, and Christian Heritage. Our books reflect our conviction that God's Word is reliable and that Jesus is the way to know Him, and live for ever with Him.

Our children's publication list covers pre-school to early teens. We also publish personal and family devotionals, biographies and inspirational stories that children will love.

From pre-school board books to teenage apologetics, we have it covered!

Christian Focus Publications Ltd,
Geanies House, Fearn, Ross-shire,
IV20 1TW, Scotland,
United Kingdom.
www.christianfocus.com

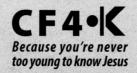